INSECTS

by
John Grassy

Scientific Consultant:
Edward M. Spevak
Curator in Charge of Invertebrates
Wildlife Conservation Society/Bronx Zoo

Kidsbooks®

Copyright © 1999, 2008, 2010 Kidsbooks, LLC
3535 West Peterson Avenue
Chicago, IL 60659

Printed in China
021001001SZ

Visit us at **www.kidsbooks.com**®

CONTENTS

THE WONDER OF INSECTS

We live in a world of insects. Close to one million different species have been identified, making them the most abundant group of creatures on earth. From flies and bees to butterflies, ants, and beetles, insects are found all over the world. One acre of ground may be home to more than a million insects!

ANCIENT INSECTS ▲

Insects have been on Earth for more than 300 million years—since before the days of the dinosaurs! We have found insect fossils (like these termites, trapped in amber) from long ago. Insects were the first creatures to develop wings and fly, which helped them escape from predators and find new places to live.

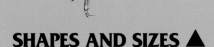

SHAPES AND SIZES ▲

Some insects are so tiny that you need a magnifying glass or microscope to get a good look at them. Unmagnified, the flea above is just 1/16 of an inch long. Other insects are huge: The African giant swallowtail butterfly is as big as a bird, with a wingspan of six to ten inches.

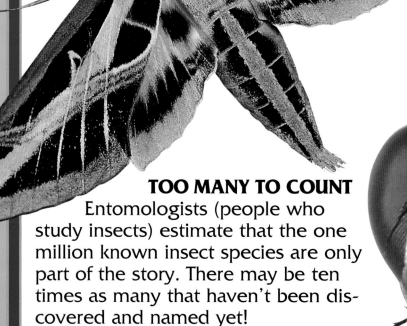

▼ This insect's name is the banded sphinx moth, or *Eumorpha fasciata*.

TOO MANY TO COUNT

Entomologists (people who study insects) estimate that the one million known insect species are only part of the story. There may be ten times as many that haven't been discovered and named yet!

ALL OVER THE WORLD

Insects live everywhere: at the frozen North and South poles and in blazing-hot deserts; in rivers and lakes; in rain forests and farm fields—even in the biggest cities. Tropical areas are home to many of the largest beetles, butterflies, and ants.

INSECTS AND PEOPLE
People have been fascinated by insects for a long time. Some we don't like—and some we do! In Japan and China, the symbol for *ant* comes from two other symbols: one that means *insect*, and one that means *unselfishness*, *justice*, and *courtesy*.

▼ Nobody likes flies, which is probably why we say "Buzz off!" to someone who is *bugging* us!

HEY, I'M FLEXIBLE ▶
Insects are experts at finding the right places to live, hide, and eat. Leaf-cutter ants (right) eat fungus that they cultivate on leaves in warm, moist places. They thrive in tropical rain forests. Carpenter ants prefer dry, soft wood, so they are much happier in older, drier forests—or the walls of your house.

▲ AMAZING COLORS
Some of the coolest colors on any living thing belong to beetles. Just look at this rainbow wood-borer! In the Amazon rain forest and elsewhere, people use the colorful outer wing cases of jewel beetles to make necklaces and other jewelry.

INSECTS IN THE WEB OF LIFE

Only one percent of all insects are the pesky kind that cause problems. What do all the others do? In nature all living things are part of the food chain. Insects are a major source of food for millions of different animal species. They do other important work, too.

▲ POLLINATORS

Lots of plants reproduce by making flowers—but the flowers can't make seeds until they get pollinated. Bees, butterflies, moths, and some beetles are pollinators: When they visit a flower to eat, they get covered with pollen, a soft powdery substance. They spread it as they go from flower to flower.

▲ RECYCLERS

Carrion beetles feed on yucky stuff, such as dead animals, fur, and feathers. They help prevent the spread of disease by turning waste materials into fresh new soil that is rich in nutrients. This helps plants grow, making food for other animals.

FISH FOOD

Water bugs, caddis flies, mayflies, and other insects live in or around water. They make great meals for all kinds of fish, as well as for frogs, salamanders, snakes, and other animals that live in or close to streams and lakes.

Giant water bugs carrying their eggs on their back.

8

BIRD FOOD ▶

Insects are food for many of the world's birds. Some swallows and warblers live on nothing but insects. It takes a lot of flies, gnats, and caterpillars to feed a nest of hungry babies, but there are always plenty of insects to go around! One third of all bird species would die off if there were no insects to eat.

▼ BUG EAT BUG

Insects are an important source of food for many animals, including other insects! Ladybugs feed on aphids; hornets and wasps eat caterpillars; ants eat the larvae of beetles and termites; and dragonflies zoom around catching gnats and mosquitoes.

BEAR FOOD

Can you believe that a 500-pound grizzly bear would eat moths? Every summer in some areas of the Rocky Mountains, grizzlies feast on hordes of army cutworm moths, scooping them up in big bunches with their paws. The moths are around for only a few weeks, so the bears gobble up all they can!

▼ YOU AND ONLY YOU

The flower on red clover is so big that most pollinators can't reach its nectar. But a bumblebee has the right stuff. Its massive body lets it burrow all the way in. The bee collects pollen and helps the clover reproduce. This is a special connection in nature between one kind of insect and one kind of plant.

9

INSECT EQUIPMENT

What makes an insect an insect? How can you distinguish insects from other creepy crawlies? It's not so hard. All of the world's insects have a few things in common.

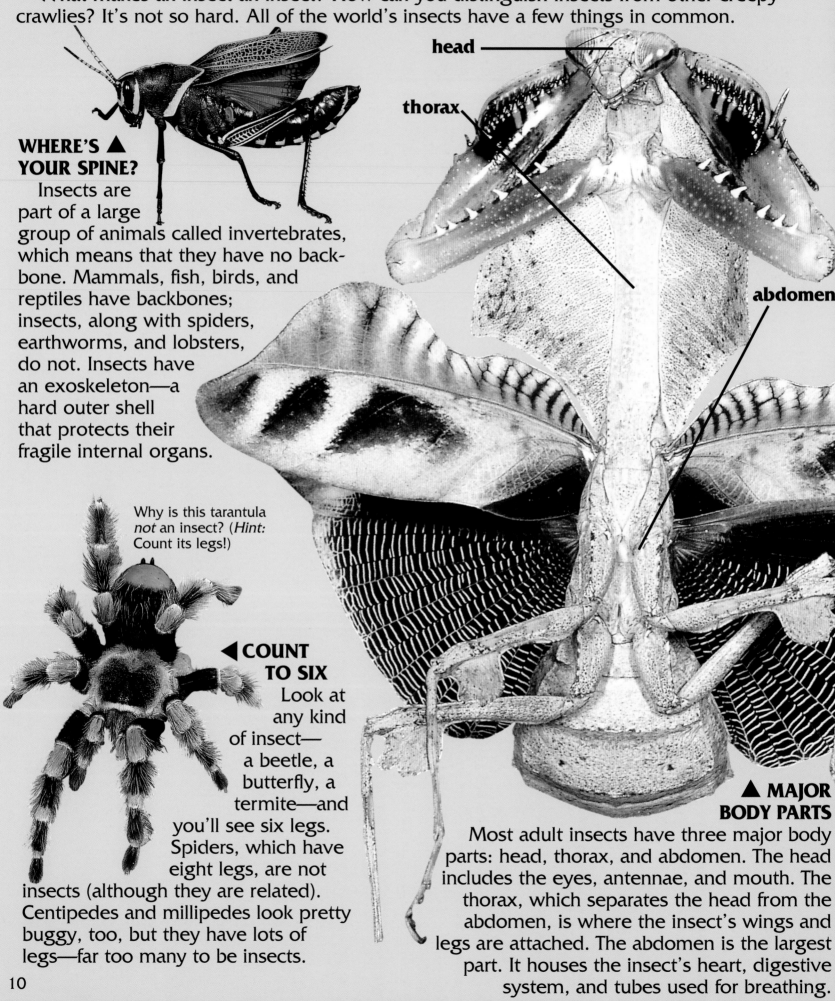

head

thorax

abdomen

WHERE'S ▲ YOUR SPINE?

Insects are part of a large group of animals called invertebrates, which means that they have no backbone. Mammals, fish, birds, and reptiles have backbones; insects, along with spiders, earthworms, and lobsters, do not. Insects have an exoskeleton—a hard outer shell that protects their fragile internal organs.

Why is this tarantula *not* an insect? (*Hint:* Count its legs!)

◄COUNT TO SIX

Look at any kind of insect— a beetle, a butterfly, a termite—and you'll see six legs. Spiders, which have eight legs, are not insects (although they are related). Centipedes and millipedes look pretty buggy, too, but they have lots of legs—far too many to be insects.

▲ MAJOR BODY PARTS

Most adult insects have three major body parts: head, thorax, and abdomen. The head includes the eyes, antennae, and mouth. The thorax, which separates the head from the abdomen, is where the insect's wings and legs are attached. The abdomen is the largest part. It houses the insect's heart, digestive system, and tubes used for breathing.

◄ EVERY BREATH YOU TAKE

Insects breathe air like other animals, but the way they do it is pretty different. Along the outside of the abdomen are tiny holes called spiracles. They allow air to flow inside the body. Connected to the spiracles are large air sacs and a web of breathing tubes called trachea (TRAY-key-uh).

WINGED WONDERS ▶

Nearly all insects have two pairs of wings. (Flies have only one pair.) Flying allows insects to travel, sometimes for hundreds or thousands of miles. This helps them find new places where food is abundant, find mates for breeding, and escape from predators and harsh weather.

A long-horned beetle about to take flight.

WEIRD BLOOD

Insects have blood (called hemolymph), but it's very different from ours. Usually, it is clear or light green in color. The insect's heart pumps blood, but the blood doesn't flow through arteries or veins, because there aren't any! It just flows freely inside the insect's body.

◄ UP FOR GRABS

The mouth of an insect is adapted to whatever that species eats—whether it chews leaves, sweeps the water for microscopic plants and animals, grabs and cuts into large prey, or bores into the tough wood of trees.

A long-horned wood-borer beetle.

11

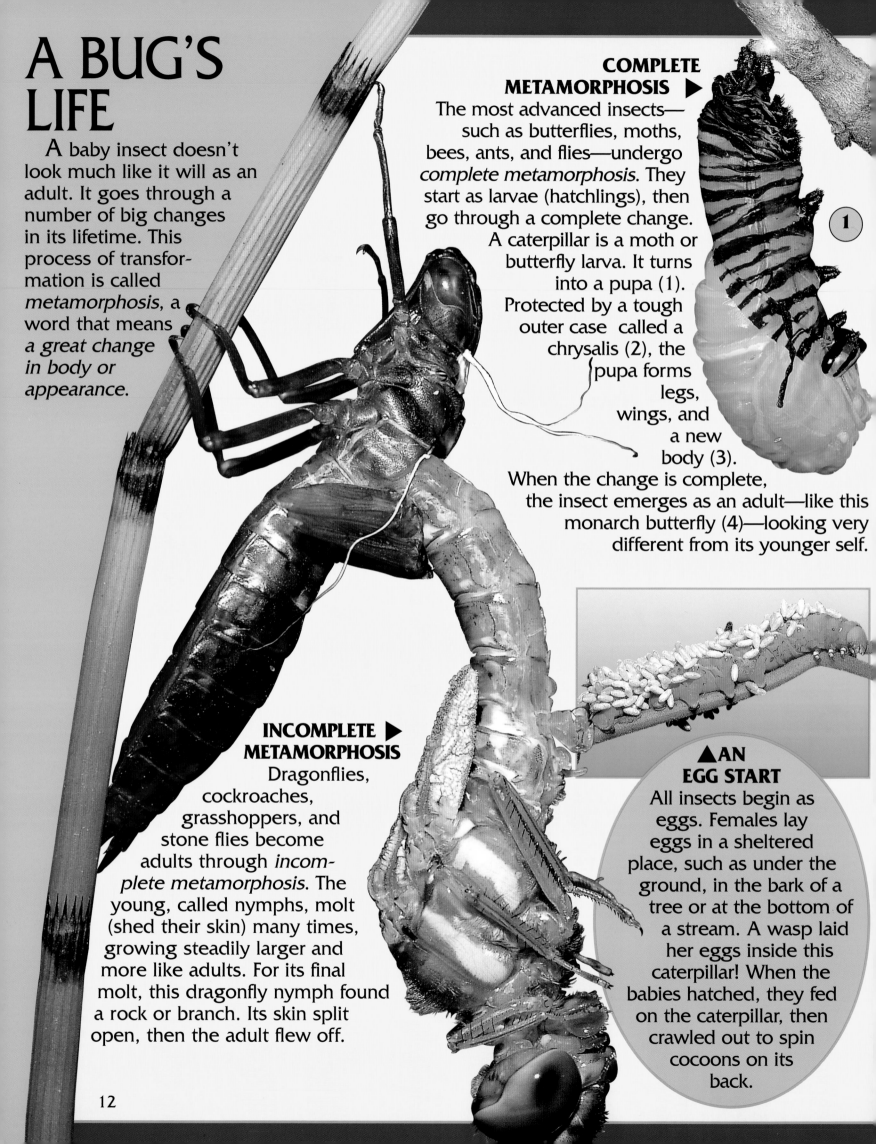

A BUG'S LIFE

A baby insect doesn't look much like it will as an adult. It goes through a number of big changes in its lifetime. This process of transformation is called *metamorphosis*, a word that means *a great change in body or appearance.*

COMPLETE METAMORPHOSIS ▶

The most advanced insects—such as butterflies, moths, bees, ants, and flies—undergo *complete metamorphosis.* They start as larvae (hatchlings), then go through a complete change. A caterpillar is a moth or butterfly larva. It turns into a pupa (1). Protected by a tough outer case called a chrysalis (2), the pupa forms legs, wings, and a new body (3). When the change is complete, the insect emerges as an adult—like this monarch butterfly (4)—looking very different from its younger self.

1

INCOMPLETE ▶ METAMORPHOSIS

Dragonflies, cockroaches, grasshoppers, and stone flies become adults through *incomplete metamorphosis.* The young, called nymphs, molt (shed their skin) many times, growing steadily larger and more like adults. For its final molt, this dragonfly nymph found a rock or branch. Its skin split open, then the adult flew off.

▲AN EGG START

All insects begin as eggs. Females lay eggs in a sheltered place, such as under the ground, in the bark of a tree or at the bottom of a stream. A wasp laid her eggs inside this caterpillar! When the babies hatched, they fed on the caterpillar, then crawled out to spin cocoons on its back.

②

③

④

1 New pupa
2 Chrysalis (KRIS-uh-lus)
3 Pupa nearing molt
4 Adult emerging

Praying mantis hatch-lings

◀ WHERE ARE MOM AND DAD?

Most insects grow up without parents around—they hatch and are soon on their way! But termites, ants, some wasps, and honeybees build large nests with special rooms for laying eggs, and spend a lot of time caring for their young. Some beetles also care for their eggs and newly hatched babies.

13

BUTTERFLIES AND MOTHS

With their awesome colors, shapes and sizes, butterflies and moths are some of the neatest insects around. You know that it's summer when you see them floating over flower gardens, ponds, and fields.

Sheep moth

▲ MOTH OR BUTTERFLY? ▼

How can you tell a moth from a butterfly? Moth antennae are lined with feathery hairs and have no club at the end; butterfly antennae have a small knob at the end. Moths rest with their wings out flat or angled like a tent; when butterflies rest, they fold their wings straight up.

California sisters butterfly

WILD BEAUTIES ▲

There are more than 170,000 kinds of butterflies and moths. They live just about everywhere, from high mountain meadows and cold, windy tundra to tropical rain forests, deserts, and woodlands. These monarch butterflies travel thousands of miles a year: They spend the summer in central and eastern North America, then fly to Mexico for the winter.

DANGEROUS COLORS ▲

Some animals eat butterflies and moths. They have to be careful, though, because some are poisonous. Most poisonous butterflies and moths have bright colors or large eyespots on their wings: warning signs that say *Danger! Stay away!* Some nonpoisonous ones have the same patterns to make other animals think that they, too, are deadly!

▲ WHAT'S IN A WING?

Butterfly and moth wings are made of tiny scales that overlap like shingles on a house. Some scales contain pigments that give moths and butterflies their incredible colors.

SUPER SIPPERS ▶

Adult moths and butterflies don't eat— they drink. They have a flexible, hollow tube, called a proboscis, for a mouth. They extend the proboscis into a flower's blossom, find the nectar, and drink it up, the way you use a straw.

HUNTERS AND HUNTED

Every single day, an insect must find enough food while making sure that other animals don't feed on it! But insects have been playing this game for millions of years, and have developed a lot of tricks to help them survive.

WHO GOES THERE?

Many mild-mannered insects have colors and shapes that make them look danger-ous—a trick called mimicry. This dead-ly-looking "snake" is really a cleverly disguised caterpillar.

▲ SPEED DEMON

The dragonfly is the fastest flier and has the keenest vision of any insect. It can see in almost every direction at once, and keeps its huge eyes clean by using special brushes on its front legs. Zooming after mayflies, mosquitoes, and other small insects, a dragonfly can hit 60 miles per hour! Male dragon-flies establish territories and will dive-bomb other males that get too close.

▲ ON THE PROWL

The front legs of the praying mantis, or mantid, are serrated for extra gripping power, to hold prey caught in its lightning-fast strike. Its head swivels in every direction, giving it excellent vision. Green or brown mantids blend with their surroundings, but the extra-tricky orchid mantid looks like a flower, drawing other bugs to its clutches.

BARK? TWIG? BUG? ►

When this northern walkingstick stops moving, it looks like a twig, blending with its surroundings. Moths and butterflies have wing colors that match the leaves or bark of trees—even the shapes of some leaves! When they sit still, birds, rodents, and other predators can't see them!

If a young walkingstick loses a leg, it grows a new one when it molts!

◄ ROW, ROW, ROW

Water striders stay afloat on long legs coated with waxy, waterproof hairs, and use their middle legs like oars to move across water. They live on ponds, rivers, or oceans, eating insects that they find on the water's surface. (They eat each other, too!) They inject their prey with an enzyme that turns its head into mush.

◄ GET OUT OF THE WAY!

When a colony of driver ants swarms through the African forest on a hunting trip, even monkeys and snakes get out of their way! The worker ants kill and devour caterpillars, scorpions, cockroaches, as well as other ants. They are the most ferocious insects in the world, even attacking much larger prey!

This katydid's bigger-than-usual face helps scare away predators.

17

SEEING, HEARING, SMELLING

Nearly all insects have eyes and ears. Though seeing and hearing are useful, taste and smell are an insect's most important senses. Insects taste and smell the air, ground, and leaves and flowers of plants in order to determine what is and is not safe to eat.

ON YOUR TRAIL ▼

When most ants leave the colony to search for food, they leave a scent trail. The ant touches its abdomen to the ground, releasing a chemical that other ants read with their antennae. Usually, the trail leads to a new source of food—or back home.

▲ A BUG'S-EYE VIEW

Most insects have two large compound eyes, plus three smaller, simple eyes on top of their head. The compound eyes contain hundreds of individual eyes, called facets. Each facet gives the insect a separate picture of the world. You can see the many facets in this fly's eyes (magnified even more in the background photo).

◄ I HEAR YOU CALLING

Hearing is all-important for katydids. There are more than 100 types of katydids in North America and each has its own song, made by rubbing its wings together. Usually, only the males sing. They sing when it's time to mate, to help females find them.

GET THE PICTURE? ▼

The range of colors that many insects see is much different from what humans see. Insects can see ultraviolet, a color that is invisible to us. This may help a bee find the right flowers to feed on, or enable a bluebottle fly to find a mate.

▲ GOOD VIBRATIONS

The cricket has an ear on each front knee! Cricket ears work much like ours: An eardrum picks up vibrations in the air. Other insects have tiny hairs around the eyes and along the body that are sensitive to air movements and other changes in their surroundings.

SHOW ME THE WAY

Fireflies are beetles, not flies. On late summer evenings, firefly males and females put on a show as they locate one another for mating. The male goes first: He sends out a pattern of flashes as he flies, then waits for a female to reply. The light is produced by special cells in the firefly's abdomen.

SNIFFING AROUND

Insects with sharp eyes, such as wasps and dragonflies, have short antennae. Others, such as some beetles and moths (like this luna moth), have long antennae covered with tiny hairs. The antennae pick up smells in the air— from as far as 10 or 12 miles away! That makes smelling as good as seeing: They can find food, safety, and mates by smelling them!

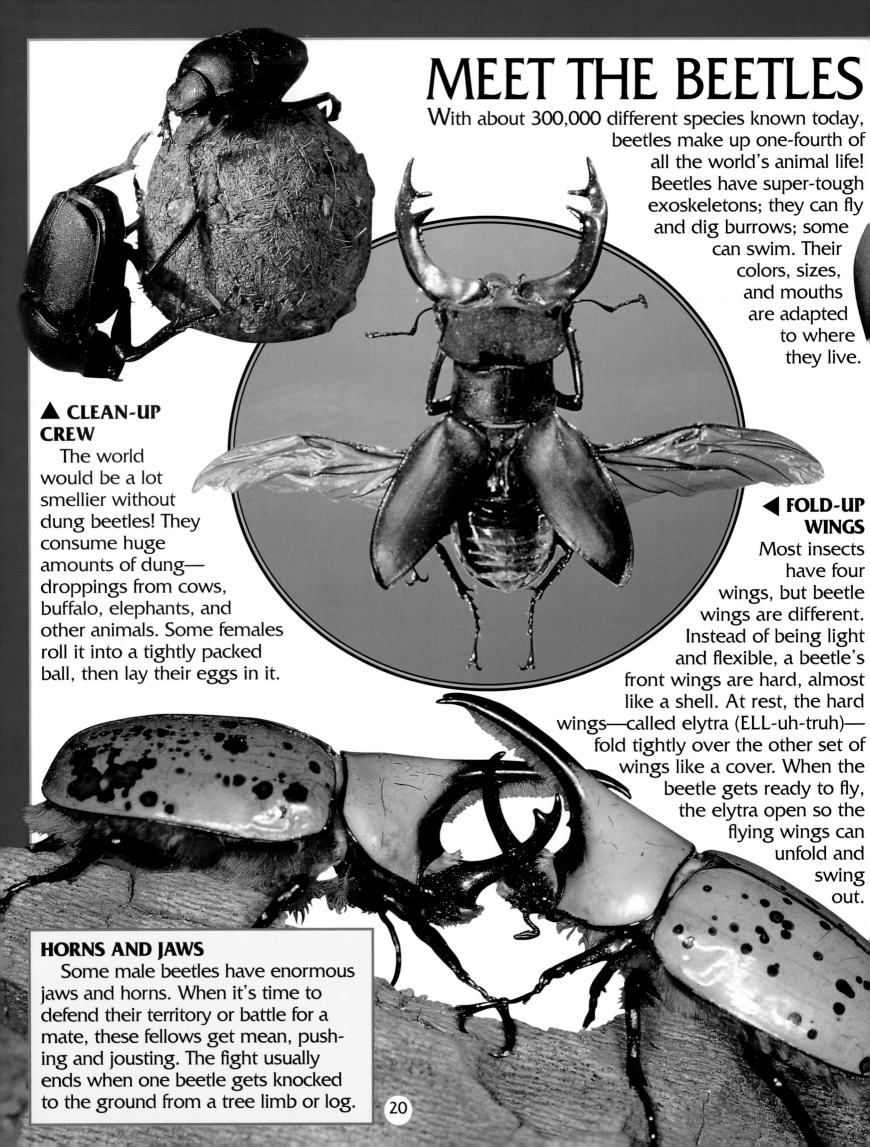

MEET THE BEETLES

With about 300,000 different species known today, beetles make up one-fourth of all the world's animal life! Beetles have super-tough exoskeletons; they can fly and dig burrows; some can swim. Their colors, sizes, and mouths are adapted to where they live.

▲ CLEAN-UP CREW

The world would be a lot smellier without dung beetles! They consume huge amounts of dung—droppings from cows, buffalo, elephants, and other animals. Some females roll it into a tightly packed ball, then lay their eggs in it.

◄ FOLD-UP WINGS

Most insects have four wings, but beetle wings are different. Instead of being light and flexible, a beetle's front wings are hard, almost like a shell. At rest, the hard wings—called elytra (ELL-uh-truh)—fold tightly over the other set of wings like a cover. When the beetle gets ready to fly, the elytra open so the flying wings can unfold and swing out.

HORNS AND JAWS

Some male beetles have enormous jaws and horns. When it's time to defend their territory or battle for a mate, these fellows get mean, pushing and jousting. The fight usually ends when one beetle gets knocked to the ground from a tree limb or log.

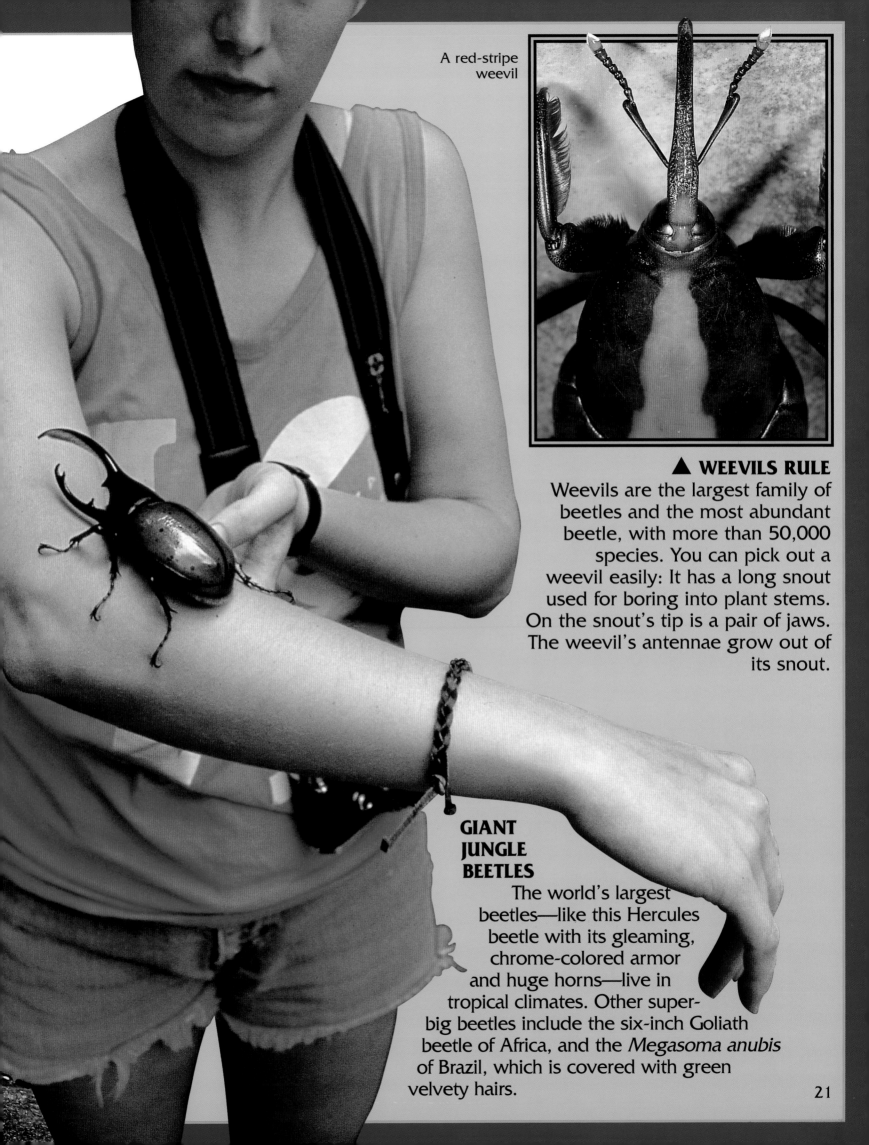

A red-stripe weevil

▲ WEEVILS RULE

Weevils are the largest family of beetles and the most abundant beetle, with more than 50,000 species. You can pick out a weevil easily: It has a long snout used for boring into plant stems. On the snout's tip is a pair of jaws. The weevil's antennae grow out of its snout.

GIANT JUNGLE BEETLES

The world's largest beetles—like this Hercules beetle with its gleaming, chrome-colored armor and huge horns—live in tropical climates. Other super-big beetles include the six-inch Goliath beetle of Africa, and the *Megasoma anubis* of Brazil, which is covered with green velvety hairs.

21

SOCIAL INSECTS

Most insects live on their own, coming together only when it's time to mate. But ants, honeybees, some wasps and hornets, and termites are social insects. They build large colonies, and each member has a job to do.

PAPIER-MÂCHÉ

A single paper-wasp queen starts a new colony each year. She chews up softened wood to make a soft, papier-mâché-like material for the nest. She lays eggs and raises the first worker wasps on her own. Then the workers, all females, take over. On hot days, they cool the nest by fanning their wings, or collecting water to spread over eggs and larvae.

SHAKE IT! ▶

Social insects need to know many things, such as where food is and whether danger is near. Honeybees perform a "dance" to let other worker bees know where nectar is. The dance provides important information—such as the direction, distance, and quantity of the nectar source.

DEFENDING THE COLONY ▶

For insects, protecting eggs and larvae from danger is job #1. If a predator threatens, worker ants scoop up their offspring and race off while soldier ants attack with biting jaws. Some soldier termites squirt a sticky goo at their enemies. Wasps and hornets swarm and sting when they smell an attack hormone released by other workers. *Yeeoww!*

▲ ALL HAIL THE QUEEN

All social insect colonies have a queen. Usually, she is larger than other members of the colony, and the only one able to lay eggs. The termite queen's abdomen becomes so swollen with eggs that she can hardly move!

HIGH-RISE HOMES

Compass termites live in Australia. They build huge, wedge-shaped mounds using soil and their own sticky secretions. Some of these towers stand 15 feet or higher and are just about waterproof. The narrow ends at the top of each mound always face north and south. If you're lost in the Australian outback, find one of these mounds and use it like a compass!

GOOD AND BAD INSECTS

There are many kinds of helpful insects. Bees produce honey and wax, silkmoth caterpillars make silk for clothing, and—for some people—insects make a nutritious, good-tasting meal! There are bad-guy bugs, too: a few kinds that make plenty of trouble for humans. It's never easy to stop them, but we keep trying!

TIMBER!

Many kinds of insects—including grasshoppers (pictured), beetles, and moths—eat the bark, leaves, and wood of trees. The larvae of spruce and pine beetles (called grubs) bore into the trunk of a living tree, weakening or killing it. Grasshoppers are defoliators, which means that they eat a tree's leaves, not the bark or wood.

STRANGE FRUIT ▲

The tiny fruit fly is one of the biggest pests in the world. Females lay eggs beneath the skin of fruits and vegetables. The larvae, called maggots, hatch soon after. The Mexican fruit fly attacks 50 different kinds of fruits and vegetables; the Mediterranean fruit fly attacks more than 250!

GOT SILK? ▶

Ever wonder why silk costs so much? It comes from specially bred and fed silkworms. Each silkworm cocoon is made of a single thread about 1,000 yards long. That thread must be carefully unwound and processed.

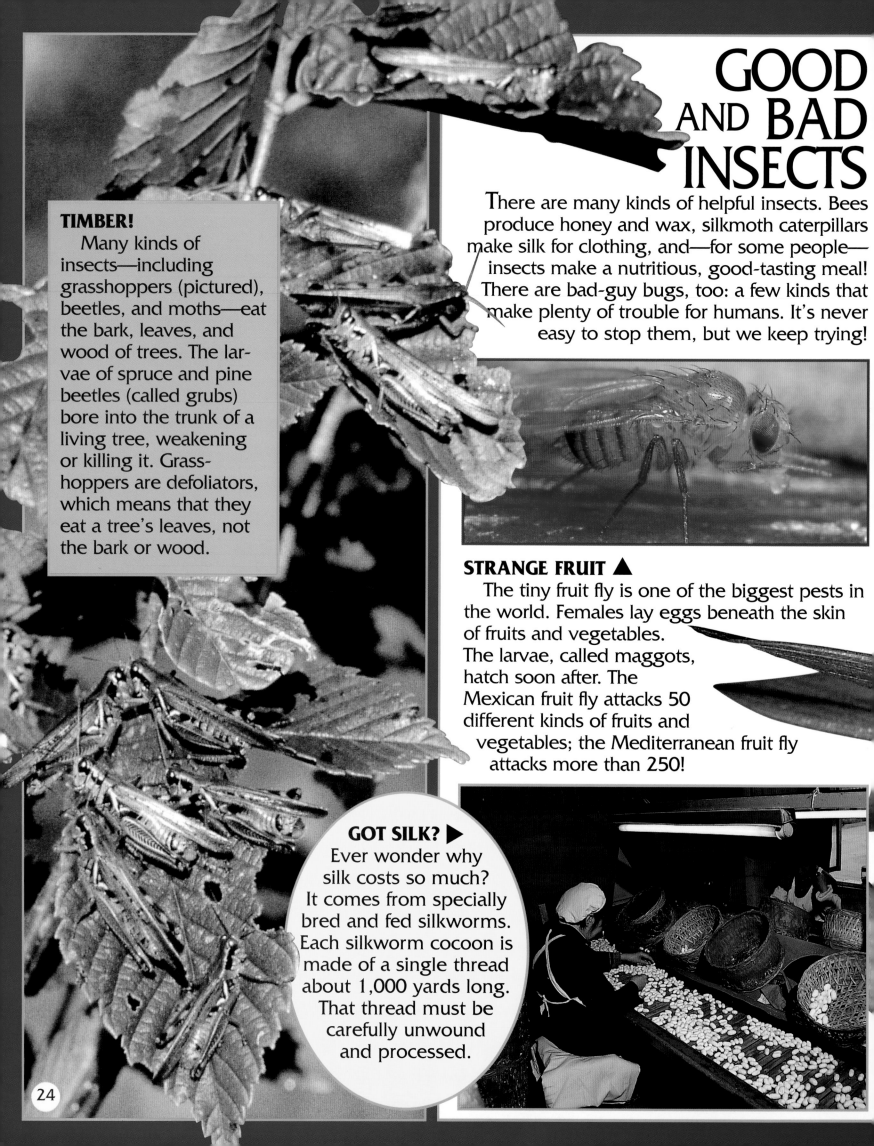

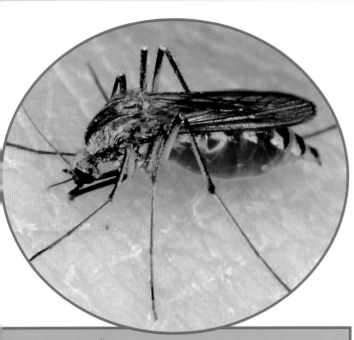

AS BUSY AS CAN BEE
From morning until dusk in summer, honeybees visit flowers. A single bee makes as many as 24 trips a day, and must stop at 100 to 1,500 flowers to fill itself with nectar. A fully loaded bee carries enough nectar to make one drop from an eyedropper. With enough bees, it all adds up: Two hives can make 150 pounds of honey in a year.

BUZZZZ ▲
There are more than 2,500 kinds of mosquitoes. Male mosquitoes eat nectar; only females drink blood. Besides spoiling outdoor fun, their bite can spread such fatal diseases as malaria and yellow fever to humans.

MAY I HELP YOU? ▶
Praying mantises help us out by doing what comes naturally—eating other bugs. The ones they like to eat are usually the same kinds that wreck crops and gardens. (They also enjoy a tasty lizard or frog now and then!)

INSECTS GET AROUND!

Insects are always looking for new places to live. They get into clothes and food shipments, airplanes and boats, luggage and boxes. Wherever people go, insects go, too. There is no way to stop them.

COTTON MENACE ▼

The boll weevil entered Texas (from Mexico) in 1892 and expanded its range by 60 miles each year. By 1922, it was destroying cotton fields throughout Alabama, Georgia, and other southeastern states. But it's a hero in Enterprise, Alabama: A statue honors it for forcing farmers there to switch to crops that turned out to be more profitable.

◄ PEST FROM OUT WEST

Long ago, the Colorado potato beetle ate only wild plants. But when American settlers moved west and began farming, it switched to the leaves of potato and tomato crops. No bug-killing chemical has stopped it yet. The beetle has taken hold across Europe and Asia, and recently showed up in China and Iran.

▲ FROM CANADA

European skipper butter-flies came to the U.S. from Canada about 80 years ago. You can now find their plump, furry bodies and brown-orange wings throughout New England. Another new population is grow-ing out west in Colorado and British Columbia. Butterfly experts believe that they may have hitched a ride on a shipment of hay.

NO KILLERS ▼

"Killer bees" are really African honeybees. Beekeepers took them to Brazil—then they escaped, breeding with other bees as they moved north. African bees are quick to defend their hives, but rarely attack people. Africanized bees make great honey. If you have a jar of honey at home, there's a good chance it was made by them.

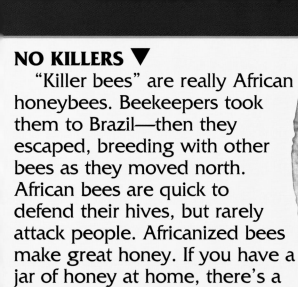

THE CITY PEST ▼

Cockroaches, also called palmetto bugs, have been around for 280 million years. They are so tough that one can live for nearly three days *without its head*! Cockroaches live by the millions in urban areas, feeding on food scraps and other debris. They are *very* fast and can squeeze into the smallest spaces.

THEY'RE EVERYWHERE

The cabbage butterfly is now so plentiful in the U.S. that it's hard to believe it's a relative newcomer. A native of England, it somehow got to Canada, where it took wing and spread throughout North America. The caterpillars feed on sour-tasting stuff—cabbage, peppergrass, and wild mustard—so it's no wonder birds don't like to eat them!

A BALANCING ACT

The natural world is one big balancing act—and insects are a vital part of it. Studying insects is a great way to learn about nature, because insects are easy to find. Be a bug detective: All you need is a jar with a lid, a magnifying glass, and a pair of tweezers for holding insects you want to study.

An earwig.

A BUG EXPERIMENT

Want to find out how quickly insects adapt to change? Set a large flat rock, log, or piece of wood somewhere in your yard. Every day, go lift it up. What insects are under there? Where did they come from? How did they find out about that place? Why do they like living there?

COME AND GET IT! ▼

If you really like butterflies and want to watch them, ask your parents about planting a butterfly garden. There are certain types of flowers that butterflies can't resist—ask at a garden store. Plant a few of them, then see how many kinds of butterflies visit.

OUR CHANGING WORLD ▲

Many insects have adapted to one kind of *habitat* (natural home). People need homes, too, so every year a little more of the world's rain forests are cleared away. Birds, insects, and other rain-forest animals become extinct—and we lose some of what helps to preserve a delicate balance.

LEARNING MORE ▲

Almost everyone knows what a cockroach looks like, but what about a tiger beetle (above) or a camel cricket? If you want to learn more about insects, buy a field identification guide. You'll see pictures of insects that live in your area, along with notes on where they live and what they eat.

OUT OF BALANCE

Why is it so hard to keep insects from damaging crops? Because a field of crops isn't like a forest or meadow, where many different plants and animals live. A crop field has just one kind of plant and few animals. If a bad bug moves in, there are often no predators to eat it—and no other kinds of plants for that bug to eat. Crop fields don't have balance.

KEEPING THE BALANCE

Why care about insects—yellow jackets like these, for instance? Without these wasps to eat caterpillars, we might not have some of our favorite flowers, because the caterpillars would destroy them. We need many different kinds of plants and animals to keep nature in balance.

29

GLOSSARY

Amber: A hard, yellowish, see-through substance made of fossilized tree resin.

Antennae: Segmented sense organs, attached to an insect's head, that help it smell and touch.

Carrion: The rotting flesh of a dead animal. (Carrion beetles feed on dead animals, fur, and feathers.)

Chrysalis: The hardened shell that a caterpillar creates around itself as it attaches itself to a tree limb or other structure and begins the process of metamorphosis (transformation) into a butterfly.

Cocoon: The protective covering spun by the larva of an insect before it undergoes metamorphosis, or transformation, into its adult form.

Defoliator: Insects, such as certain caterpillars, that eat a tree's leaves but not its bark or wood.

Elytra: The hard front wings of a beetle. The elytra fold tightly over the other set of wings like a cover.

Entomologist: Scientist who studies insects.

Exoskeleton: A hard, outer skeleton or shell that protects an insect's fragile internal organs.

Facets: The hundreds of eyes contained in the compound eyes of an insect.

Fossil: The remains or impression of an animal or plant naturally preserved in rock or other hard substances.

Fungus: Any member of the group of organisms called fungi, such as mold, rust, and mushrooms.

Habitat: The area where an animal or plant naturally lives and grows.

Hemolymph: The blood of insects and other invertebrate animals.

Invertebrates: Animals that do not have backbones—such as insects, spiders, and earthworms.

Larva: A hatchling insect that does not look like its parents. After feeding and growing, larvae metamorphose into adult forms that do resemble their parents.

Metamorphosis: The changes in form during the life of an animal. Larvae, such as caterpillars, metamorphose into butterflies or moths.

Mimicry: The resemblance of a living creature to some other thing, such as a branch, flower, rock, or other animal, so as to deceive prey or predators.

Nectar: The sweet liquid of certain plants, used to make honey.

Nymph: A young insect that becomes adult through incomplete metamorphosis, molting many times until it resembles its parents.

Pollination: The process of fertilizing a plant. Bees, butterflies, moths, and some beetles pollinate flowers by spreading pollen from flower to flower.

Predator: An animal that hunts other animals for food.

Proboscis: The flexible, hollow tube that serves as a butterfly's mouth.

Pupa: The stage between larva and adult of a metamorphic insect, when legs, wings, and a new body are formed.

Serrated: Having a notched edge, like on a saw or steak knife. (The serrated front legs of the praying mantis give it extra gripping power.)

Species: A group of animals that mate and produce offspring with each other but do not breed with animals of another group; an animal belonging to a biological classification.

Spiracle: A breathing hole along the outside of an insect's abdomen that allows air to flow inside the body.

Thorax: The middle of the three sections of an insect's body, where wings and legs are located.

Trachea: Breathing tubes located in an insect's abdomen that make up its respiratory system.

Wingspan: The distance from the tip of one of a pair of wings to the tip of the other.